21st CENTURY CLARINET SE

PEPITA GREUS

Pascual Pérez Choví

Arranged for Clarinet and Piano (with optional Castanets) by
Paula Corley

PIANO

keisersouthernmusic.com

PERFORMANCE NOTES

Pascual Pérez Choví was born in a Province of Valencia, Spain, in 1889. He began his clarinet and music theory studies at age 7 with the director of the Municipal Band of Valencia. Four years later, he became the E-flat clarinet soloist with the band and later the principal B-flat clarinetist. Choví eventually became the director of the Alginet Musical Art Society Band, with whom he conducted the premier of *Pepita Greus*. The piece is dedicated to Angela-Josefa Greus Saez whose nickname was "Pepita." Chovi had a crush on Pepita, but her family forbid their romance. She eventually became a nun.

Pepita Greus is a pasadoble (meaning "double step" in Spanish), which is a dramatic Latin dance based on the sound, drama, and movement of the Spanish bullfight. However, the piece is presented in common march form. The opening fanfare leads to the first strain in a minor key, followed by the second strain in relative major. The trio begins quietly with a delicate melody before featuring the solo clarinet on the repeat. The "break strain" appears before a strong finish that features both clarinet and piano in a melodic exchange. This arrangement for clarinet, piano, and castanets presents the original solo clarinet part with a piano reduction of the band accompaniment and optional castanet part.

Pepita Greus

Pasadoble for Clarinet and Piano
with optional Castanets

Pascual Pérez Choví
arranged by Paula Corley

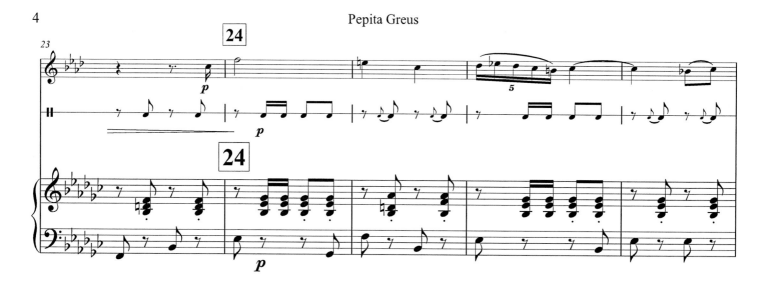

Pepita Greus

Pepita Greus

Pasadoble for Clarinet and Piano
with optional Castanets

Clarinet in B♭

Pascual Pérez Choví
arranged by Paula Corley

Clarinet in B♭

PEPITA GREUS

Pascual Pérez Choví

Arranged for Clarinet and Piano (with optional Castanets) by

Paula Corley

CASTANETS

keisersouthernmusic.com

Pepita Greus
Pasadoble for Clarinet and Piano
with optional Castanets

Pascual Pérez Choví
arranged by Paula Corley

Castanets

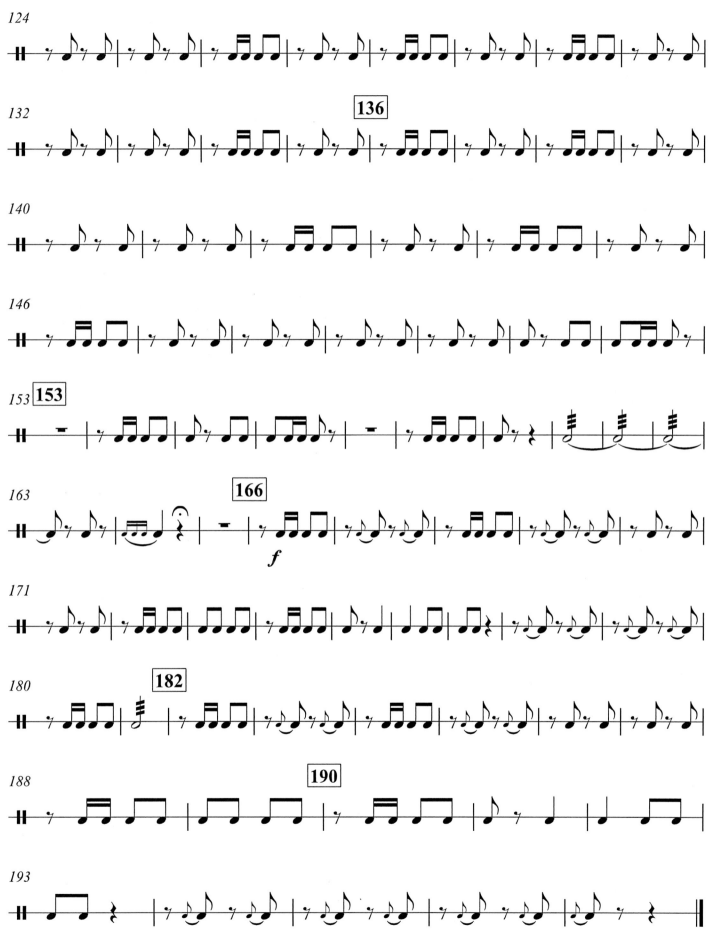

V.S.

Clarinet in B♭

optional 8va

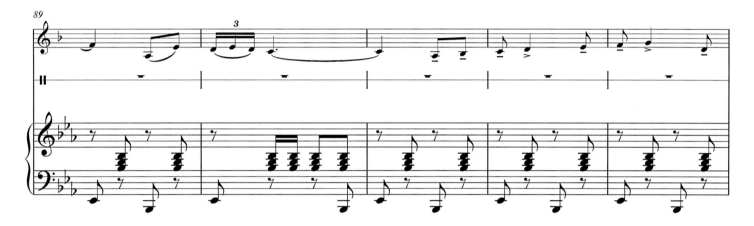

Pepita Greus

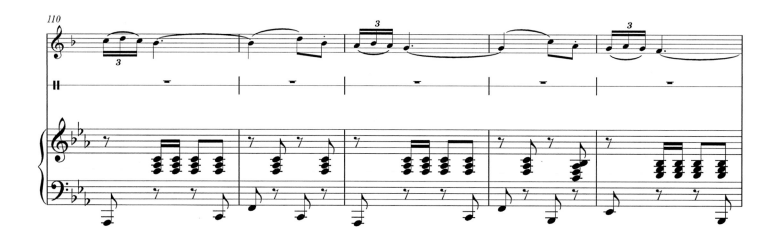

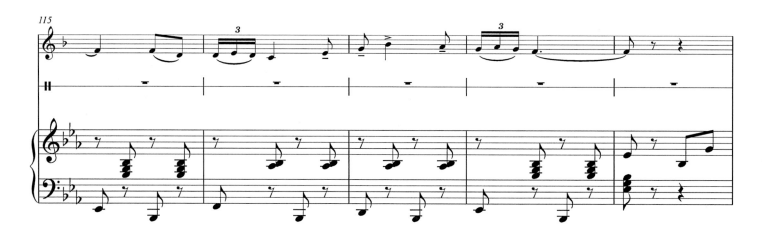

Pepita Greus

Keiser Southern Music
Clarinet Publications

Charles Neidich
21st Century Series

BRAHMS - TWO SONATAS, Op. 120
NEW URTEXT EDITION - THE FIRST BASED ON BRAHMS' MANUSCRIPTS

This edition of the *Sonatas Op. 120 for Clarinet and Piano* is unique in that it is the first and only one based on a thorough study of Brahms' working manuscripts, which the composer generally destroyed. These, however, he gave to his great friend, the clarinetist Richard Mühlfeldt. They include both the piano scores plus the clarinet parts written for Mühlfeldt. They not only clear up problems of where Brahms placed dynamics and expression marks, they resolve questions of misprints which have remained to this day in every edition since Simrock first published them in 1895. HL00298301

ALSO AVAILABLE

CAVALLINI 30 Caprices for Clarinet "the only edition with audio"*	42367
GERSHWIN Three Preludes for Clarinet and Piano	144422
JEANJEAN 18 Etudes for Clarinet*	42385
MOZART Concerto in A Major KV. 622	172779
ROSSINI Introduction, Theme and Variations	111949
WEBER Concertino for Clarinet and Piano	111948

*includes audio

Paula Corley
ICA Pedagogy Chair

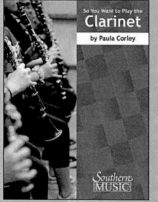

SOUTHERN MUSIC INTRODUCES TWO OUTSTANDING NEW EDUCATIONAL PUBLICATIONS

SO YOU WANT TO PLAY THE CLARINET

So You Want to Play the Clarinet is a carefully sequenced book for beginner clarinetists that emphasizes good tone quality and phrasing. The range is moderate, from the lowest E to third line B-flat. Rhythms and basic techniques needed for first semester performance are included. For the best result, follow the lessons in order. With regular practice, you can teach yourself to play. Visit clarinetcity.com to find articles, videos, and helpful information that is free to download. HL00298849

THE BREAK

Crossing the 'break' can be a source of frustration for developing clarinetists. *The Break* is a logical guide for mastering this important step in clarinet performance. Part 1 of the method covers the clarinet overtone series and how new note names attach to previously learned fingerings, the 'right hand down' technique, first scales across the break and melodies in the clarion register. Part 2 contains *Rhythmical Articulation Studies* by Pasquale Bona, selected and edited for clarinet. These combined studies and exercises provide the ideal means to develop smooth connections between the lower and middle registers of the clarinet. HL00298118

Richard Stoltzman
21st Century Series

BACH SONATA No. 2 in D MAJOR
for Viola da gamba and keyboard
NEW FIRST-EVER PUBLICATION FOR CLARINET OF THIS MASTERPIECE

Bach's *Sonata for Viola da gamba and Harpsichord, BWV 1028*, would later be incorporated into one of the composer's greatest masterpieces, the *St. Matthew's Passion*. This new transcription by Richard Stoltzman, edited for Clarinet in A, was inspired by collaborations with two legendary pianists - Keith Jarrett and Yehudi Wyner. This publication's clarinet part contains Stoltzman's performance suggestions and interpretive markings, set off in a light grey as to not alter the original. HL000262903

ALSO AVAILABLE

BACH Chromatic Fantasia and Fugue for Clarinet and Bass Clarinet Duo*	42681
BRAHMS Intermezzo, Op. 118 No. 2 for Clarinet and Piano*	42682
FOSS Elegy for Clarinet and Piano	144421
HARTKE Concerto for Clarinet: Landscape with Blues (solo/piano reduction)	127805
SCHUBERT Sonatines 1 & 2, Op. 137 for Clarinet and Piano	42593

*includes audio

ORDER TODAY
from any retailer or at HALLEONARD.COM
Visit our website: **KEISERSOUTHERNMUSIC.COM**